Weight Loss Daily Devotional & Prayer Book

KRISTEN KNIGHT

DEDICATION

This book is dedicated to all of you who are on your weight loss journey. May you feel guidance and motivation from the Lord!

Table of Contents

INTRODUCTION

Weight loss can be difficult, and we may try many diets or new fads without maintaining results.

God loves you, and wants you to be healthy so that you can walk with Him and experience the abundance of gifts He has to offer.

Don't give up yet!

13 *"May the God of hope fill you with all joy and peace as you trust in Him, so that you may overflow with hope by the power of the Holy Spirit."*

Romans 15:13

As always, now is the time to lean on God.

26 *".. With people this is impossible, but with God all things are possible."*

Matthew 19:26

Believe the unbelievable, and receive the impossible. See your potential weight loss happening for you, because all things are possible with God, we just need to lean on Him.

I this book I hope to encourage you in Christ through daily devotions and prayers based on the scriptures, to guide you on your weight loss journey and enrich your relationship with God. It aims to motivate you, and bring Gods loving gifts to realisation in your life.

Let's pound those pounds with the Word of God!

DAY 1 – ALL THINGS ARE POSSIBLE

Matthew 19:26

And looking at them Jesus said to them, "With people this is impossible, but with God all things are possible."

You have heard it a million times – All Things Are Possible Through God! But do you truly believe it?

With God, ALL things are possible. Draw near to Him, and He will draw near to you. Be guided by Him, not by the world's limits. The Lord has no limits so what are you waiting for? See things in God's reality, not your own.

The next time you catch yourself thinking 'Oh, I can't exercise,' try it anyway. You might surprise yourself and succeed, and you will definitely feel better for it afterwards. If you haven't exercised for a while – start small. Believe you can do it. Have faith as small as a mustard seed, faith that God will pull you through. Believe the unbelievable. Receive the impossible. God has made this promise, so who are you to question it?

If that piece of chocolate cake seems too hard to resist – pray! Focus your attention on Him instead.

"The godly cry out and the LORD hears; he saves them from all their troubles."

Psalm 34:17

Prayer:

Lord, remind me today that all things are possible. Help me with my weight loss journey, to deepen my faith in you and gain self-belief at the same time. I will commit to doing at least a small amount of exercise today.

DAY 2 – ENTER THROUGH THE NARROW GATE

Matthew 7:13-14

Enter through the narrow gate. For wide is the gate and broad is the road that leads to destruction and many enter through it. But small is the gate and narrow the road that leads to life, and only a few find it.

In a world where disappointment is around every corner, take the narrow gate and realize that you are entitled to miracles. In contrast to the disappointments on the broad road, every divine promise is guaranteed. Taking the narrow road is the only way to be reconciled to God—through faith in Christ, and this requires a commitment to a lifestyle of trust, love, sacrifice and dependence. We must go through Him to find life. Enter in and set your feet on the path of life.

Jesus has given us the gift of hope, and the promise of love. Focus on that hope and love today.

Fast food is a very broad gate – everybody is eating it, and it is definitely leading to destruction – obesity, diabetes, heart problems – the list goes on. Take the narrow gate by preparing your own healthy nutritious food. Only good things can come from this!

Prayer:

Lord, give me strength this day to choose the narrow path, that I may not be led astray by the broad road, and instead live according to Your will. Help me to resist the temptation of the easy way out, when I know it only leads to destruction.

DAY 3 – A NEW CREATION

2 Corinthians 5:17

Therefore, if anyone is in Christ, he is a new creation; the old has gone, the new has come!

Our past has been covered by the blood of Christ, and we have a new set of life values and goals. Everyone in Christ is a new creation. You don't have to decide to be a new creation, it doesn't say you have a choice in this. The fact is that you *are* a new creation. You may see yourself in the mirror, and see yourself larger than you would like to be. Try looking at yourself as a beautiful creation of God, who is on a journey to be healthier. You are *becoming* a new creation in Christ.

We are not subject to the worlds opinions of us. We only need to concern ourselves with how God sees us. Look at your actions, words and deeds as they are today, not as they were yesterday. What we do with Christ will determine our eternal dwelling place.

Prayer:

Lord, thank you for changing us by sacrificing Your Son Jesus Christ. Thank you for making us a new creation! Let Your love meet all of my needs, and set me free to live not for myself but to live for You.

DAY 4 – REJOICE!

Philippians 4:4-7

Rejoice in the Lord always. I will say it again: Rejoice! Let your gentleness be evident to all. The Lord is near. Do not be anxious about anything, but in everything, by prayer and petition, with thanksgiving, present your requests to God. And the peace of God, which transcends all understanding, will guard your hearts and minds in Christ Jesus.

Focus today on your 'gentleness being evident to all'. Feeling anxious? Do exactly as the scriptures say, and pray with thanksgiving. It's so simple! We don't want to ruminate on our problems, going over our issues again and again. What a waste of energy! We can hand *everything* over to God, by prayer and petition, with thanksgiving. Petition can be defined as doing something, over and over again. Everything, even the small things. God wants us to be happy, He wants us to rejoice! We can rejoice, not because life is easy, but because we know everything is in God's loving hands.

Rejoicing is a choice, it very rarely comes naturally, so fake it 'til you make it. Rejoice in the new creation you are becoming through your weight loss journey. Rejoicing can become a habit when we realise how much we have to be joyful about.

Joy is often overlooked in today's task-orientated world. Think back to the last time you enjoyed a true belly laugh, or when you were so joyful about an event in your life that you nearly burst. God is offering us the gift of joy, but this gift is rarely opened.

The definition of joy is a feeling of great pleasure and happiness. Wouldn't it be great if we experienced this every day? We can! God has given us an abundance of opportunities to be joyful, we just aren't looking for them. Look around you. What do you have to be joyful about? If you are going through trials at the moment, this task may seem difficult, but I promise you, if you think hard enough, you can find things to be grateful for and joyful about.

Prayer:

Lord, I make a commitment to hand everything over to You through prayer, so that I can spend more time rejoicing, rather than worrying.

DAY 5 – COME TO ME, ALL YOU WHO ARE WEARY AND BURDENED

Matthew 11:28-30

28 Come to me, all you who are weary and burdened, and I will give you rest.
29 Take my yoke upon you and learn from me, for I am gentle and humble in heart, and you will find rest for your souls.
30 For my yoke is easy and my burden is light.

Are you weary? One of the main causes of weariness is the burdens we carry around, they are interlinked. Burdens can be physical difficulties, emotional conflicts, loss of loved ones, financial hardship, insecurities feelings of hopelessness – the list goes on! In this day and age we are often multi-tasking, trying to achieve so much, and trying to keep everyone happy. No wonder we're weary!

Jesus promises to '.. give you rest'. He wants to give you rest, otherwise he wouldn't have offered it. Jesus isn't going to say 'Sorry, I don't feel like giving you rest today. Come back next week'. It is available for you today.
Jesus says 'Come to me, all you who are weary and burdened, and

9

I will give you rest.' Notice He says 'all', not just some, to come to Him. He gently instructs and directs and carries our burdens with us.

In Psalm 119:28 it says:

> *28 My soul is weary with sorrow;*
> *strengthen me according to your word.*

We are of no use to anybody when we are run down, burnt out and tired. We can keeping pressing on through this, putting in full effort, but we may not actually be much help at all. God wants us to rest sometimes, keep ourselves healthy, and look after ourselves. We can be a much more productive vessel for him when we are running at full capacity. Recharge your batteries. Flat batteries are of no use to anyone. Getting exercise, even when you are tired, can be a great energy boost – it gets your endorphins pumping, and your serotonin – your happy hormones – activated.

Put some time for yourself in your diary. This may just be an hour to sit down and read a book. If you have little children, you may laugh at this idea – but what about taking some time out when they go to bed instead of tidying up after them. Having some rest, and some time out for yourself will give you plenty of energy to do that in the morning – the mess won't run away. Our families will revel in our new found energy when we start practicing this, and will eventually encourage us to do it more often!

Prayer:

Lord, thank you for allowing me rest by carrying my burdens with me. Teach me to lean on You more in times of weariness.

Kristen Knight

DAY 6 – HAVE FAITH

Hebrews 11:1

Now faith is being sure of what we hope for and certain of what we do not see.

Faith is not an easy thing to describe. It is believing in the unseen, and it is the key to everything as a Christian – particularly our salvation – which we would have nothing without. This verse calls for us to be 'sure' of what we hope for, and 'certain' of what we do not see. Be sure of your weight loss, even if you can't see it yet. You know that you are on the right path, and you will continue on this path because of the hope God has given you.

Living in the love of God can help you with this, the knowing that He is there for you and loves you, no matter where you are in life. Focus on Jesus, and faith will follow. Trust in God, and His promises, and they will come to fruition.

Because you have so little faith. I tell you the truth, if you have faith as small as a mustard seed, you can say to this mountain, 'Move from here to there' and it will move. Nothing will be impossible for you.

Matthew 17:20-21

Faith is the substance of things hoped for. It is the evidence of things unseen. A mountain can be referred to as an obstruction or difficulty, and Jesus says all we need is faith as small as a mustard seed to get beyond these, moving them from our path to a life in Christ. Nothing will be impossible for you. Move this mountain called weight. You don't need to have an abundance of faith, God wants you to start with the faith you have, no matter how little that is. Trust Him to save you.

Prayer:

Lord, I place my faith in Jesus Christ. Help me in my areas of unbelief, so that I may move mountains with Your help. Help me develop my faith by trusting in You.

DAY 7 – THE BREAD OF LIFE

John 6:35

I am the bread of life. He who comes to me will never go hungry,
and he who believes in me will never be thirsty.

Bread is a staple in our diet, just as Jesus should be a staple in our spiritual diet. Focus on partaking in Him, rather than partaking in unhealthy food. If we are not partaking in Him, we will be spiritually hungry and thirsty. The moment we believe in Jesus, He delivers His promise to keep us satisfied. Just as healthy food helps our bodies grow and heal, Jesus helps our souls. Jesus is The Word, and feeding yourself with it every day will keep you spiritually strong.

But seek first His kingdom and His righteousness, and all these
things will be given to you as well. Therefore do not worry about
tomorrow, for tomorrow will worry about itself. Each day has
enough trouble of its own.

Matthew 6:33-34

Worry is contrary to faith in Christ. When you spend your energy worrying, your trust in God fades. This is no way to live if you are to be in Christ Jesus. We have a God who provides our needs day by day, and he will act to supply your needs when the time is best. Allow God to be God, have faith in Him rather than in yourself or your circumstances. *Seek first His kingdom and His righteousness, and all these things will be given to you as well.*

Prayer:

Lord, teach me to seek your kingdom, that I may not worry about tomorrow. Remind me each day to draw nearer to you through Your Word.

CONCLUSION

Remember – All things are possible through Christ who strengthens you! I wish you all the best on your weight loss journey!

If you have found this book helpful, please remember to leave a review. This will help me in writing further books on weight loss!

<u>Romans 8:26</u>

At the same time the Spirit also helps us in our weakness, because we don't know how to pray for what we need. But the Spirit intercedes along with our groans that cannot be expressed in words.

Made in the USA
Las Vegas, NV
21 May 2024